Quit

Pam
Many thanks!
Robert

Other Books by Robert Chaney

Visits to the Manger — Enlightening Parables of Spiritual Wonder

Akashic Records: Past Lives and New Directions

The Power of Your Own Medicine

Ten Steps to Self Fulfillment

The Inner Way

Mysticism — The Journey Within

Unfolding the Third Eye

Think on New Levels

The Jeweled Tree of Life

Occult Hypnotism

Reincarnation: Cycle of Opportunity

Transmutation: How the Alchemists Turned Lead into Gold

The Essenes and Their Ancient Mysteries

Quit

Alternative Methods for Overcoming Addiction

Robert Chaney

Astara's Library of Mystical Classics

Published by

Astara

792 West Arrow Highway
Upland, CA 91785

Astara, Inc.
792 W. Arrow Hwy.
P.O. Box 5003
Upland, CA 91785-5003
www.astara.org

ISBN 0-918936-44-6
Library of Congress Control Number: 2002109593

Printed in the United States of America
Cover design by Elizabeth Hickerson

Table of Contents

Dedication

This book is for that small but growing number of courageous people who are ready to take serious steps toward a victory over an addiction or compulsion, and thus regain control over their lives. They are also willing to include a spiritual dimension in any plan of therapy currently being followed.

The intent is not to replace any standard therapeutic method, but to reinforce them with an understanding of other qualities of consiousness and inner energies — and with details of how to access and use them.

Acknowledgements

A bountiful bundle of thanks goes to Steve Doolittle, Elizabeth Hickerson, Pamela Rau, Susan Chelgren, Angelica Morris, Dean Zakich, and my daughter Sita, for the skills and talents they contributed to the print and audio versions of this book. Thanks also to those who shared their own stories of overcoming addictions.

Foreword

There was a time when I didn't like myself at all. I despised myself as a spineless weakling. I had enough guts to quit — but not enough to stay quit.

My addiction was tobacco. It was easy to quit. I did it over and over. But I kept puffing and puffing. Hacking and hacking. Despising and despising.

How I finally did quit is a tangled web of causes. I'm not going to parade them for you, because it wouldn't help you. Your situation is unique. It's different than mine, different than anyone else's. Only you can put the pieces of your personal puzzle in their proper places.

For the most part, you'll find this a pretty unorthodox book. In respect to compulsions — from the mildest whims to the most frantic addictions — it might be considered as an alternative way, just as there are alternative healing therapies in modern medicine. Its purpose is to give you some non-conventional ideas and methods to supplement whatever procedures of coping you may already be using, if any. Or it may even be sufficient unto itself. Some of its theories have never been scientifically explored — which doesn't mean they might not be effective for you.

At the same time, while your addiction is highly individual and unique to your life patterns, it also bears a commonality with others'. There are similar pressures, behaviors, situations and substances — in effect, similar causes. Therefore, they yield to similar modes of coping and reversing. Outer circumstances may vary greatly; inner results are very similar.

So what I propose to do is give you lots of pieces to the puzzle, a few of mine and lots of others. You can put them together to create any picture you really want. Your choice.

Before we begin, though, I think we should agree on one thing. At your command at this moment is one of the hardest — and greatest — opportunities of a lifetime. How to quit! If you don't go for it, sooner or later you'll despise yourself as I did, and as you may already have done a hundred times or more.

If you're seriously addicted, you have only one possession left in all the world — your own potential. You may not even know what that potential is. Most have never been told. In this work, I hope to help you catch sight of it, crave it, and covet it so strongly that you're willing to do the necessary work to develop it. To conquer an addiction usually means to do as much or more to vanquish it as to sustain it.

You weren't born to be a failure. You were born to fulfill your potential. Your investment in one is about the same as the other, but the returns are as different as the bottom of a mole hole and the peak of Mt. Everest. Go for the peak experience.

Robert Chaney
Upland, California
October, 2002

One

In Whose Image Are You?

Life is a series of problems. Quitting is one problem in the series. It might even be described as a *lead problem* for it permeates and reinforces problems in a dozen other areas: relationships, careers, health, love, self-satisfaction, self-pride and the sense of accomplishment and dignity. Impulsive behavior in one area is seed for more and more compulsive behavior in the same area.

Most of us put off solving the lead problem by telling ourselves we will do so after all other problems are solved. "The big problems can wait till the smaller ones are solved. The smaller problems are easier to solve so I'll handle them first."

We fool ourselves with this type of thinking because larger problems fester at a faster rate than do the smaller, and often the smaller ones disappear when the larger are treated. No doctor avoids treating larger illnesses to treat the lesser. That would be therapy in reverse, therapy that would enlarge greater illness while working to eradicate the lesser.

Would you delay quitting an addiction to caffeine until you could conquer an addiction to heroin? Of course not. Do the larger and more damaging first. Gain your self respect at the accomplishment of eradicating the larger. Many other problems will vanish as a result.

An addict is often not a very likeable person. If you are committed to addictive behavior, give generous thanks for those who love you in spite of your problem. They sometimes do so at a great and unfair cost to themselves.

You may think of yourself as a person without value to any other person. Actually, that perspective is fostered by your addiction or compulsion. First, you are of value to humanity as a whole. And second, you are valuable to one, tens, hundreds or even more individuals. Some ideas must be taken on faith, and possibly this is one of them for you: Use the simple but effective tool of meditation.

In this context, meditation means to engage daily in a few moments (10 to 20 minutes) in a state of mental reverie. Allow thoughts to roam freely in your mind. Capture and expand upon those that offer meaningful motivations and methods that assist you on the high road to overcoming. More ideas regarding meditation are in later pages. If you would do a simple meditation upon the fact that you are valuable to one or more others, you originate a flow of positive energies and ideas into your own life that will strengthen your determination, and therefore your will, to say “No!” — Quit!

All the above indicates how important a part love plays in reaching your goal of rising to the surface of self-respect — addiction free. Addiction is based on greedy self-interest that fractures relationships. To paraphrase a statement of poet and philosopher John Donne, “No man is an island.” Neither man nor woman is an island, isolated from all others, unless he or she wills it so. Even attempting to will it so is pointless because it is impossible.

Addiction and compulsion are the barren soil in which nothing but self-interest and isolation exist. Sailing on Egypt’s Nile River reveals an illustration of this concept. Lush foliage of every imaginable type grows upon the river banks. Suddenly, the next step is into stark and unrelenting desert heat and sand in which next to nothing truly lives. In human life that is the step into addiction.

But the step back into the place where life and love abound is your choice at this moment. Choose life. Now.

Many years ago a friend and professional associate, Rev. Ruby Morrow, was in Peru at the site of Machu Picchu, meaning "old peak," the Inca holy site high in the Andes mountains. Adjoining Machu Picchu is a connecting peak named Wayna Picchu, meaning "new peak." A few of the group decided to climb Wayna Picchu, Ruby among them. She dismissed from her consciousness limitations of age and physical strength, and replaced them with strength and determination of her own will. She made the climb, the old Ruby died and a new Ruby was born.

Succumbing to addiction is one form of giving in to a limitation. Overcoming the limitation is a form of rebirth.

In life we pass through numerous cycles of death and rebirth (or reincarnations, if you prefer the term). We die as a child and are reborn as an adolescent. We die as an adolescent and are reborn as an adult. We die a slow death to addiction but are reborn as a freed individual when we overcome it. All this occurs without parameters of race, religion, politics, financial position, or parenthood. Nor any of the other criteria which are superficial creations of a humanity with its own addictive compulsion to create judgments, labels and categories of a hundred other perceptions of partial truths and total untruths. None of them are influences in your choosing to quit or not to quit. There is absolutely no valid reason whatsoever not to quit.

None. There is no power of will so weak that it cannot be invoked.

If you are to believe the movies, the Old West was filled with characters going from place to place saying, "This town ain't big enough for both of us." Then one or the other is shot.

Fortunately, unlike towns in the Old West, this world *is* big enough for all of us. This big world is really awfully small too. We're in it together. The least we can do is make the best of it. Next door, or around the globe, we're all neighbors.

Unfortunately, resembling the Old West, there are always those who would like to recreate you in their own image. They'll do most anything to accomplish their ambition, even though they may not realize that's what it is. You've heard their coaxing,

"One more won't hurt you!"

"You can always quit tomorrow!"

"It's easy. You can quit any time you want to."

"Try it. You'll really feel good."

"Everyone's doin' it. You don't want to be the only one who isn't!"

"Don't let anyone tell you what to do with your life," is the urging of someone who then proceeds to tell you what to do.

Like the Old West again, before long someone is shot, or might as well be. Each time someone urges you to "have one more," or "try it, it won't hurt you," they're challenging you to see who is stronger. Rise to the challenge — be stronger than that person, or persons, — and win! Beat the challenge. QUIT!

Why does someone want to re-create you in his or her own image? Because it's profitable!

Sometimes it's money. Sometimes it's ego. Sometimes it's power. Sometimes it's because that person literally hates to have you on any level but their own. Sometimes it's revenge. Often it's because that person hates him or herself — and the old folk saying is, "Misery loves company." But whatever the reason, one thought out of the Old West still applies today, though in a different context. This town — if by use of that word we mean your body, your family, your vocation, your life — isn't big enough to accommodate you and your negative compulsions.

There are lots of severe compulsions — substance abuse is just one of them. Not only do they require different methods of elimination, they require a combination of methods in every instance.

Sixty years ago, a traditional physician who became a non-traditional therapist, gave me a one sentence lesson from which I've made innumerable applications. He said, "Every illness results from at least three causes — and requires at least three types of treatment."

He pointed out that most malignancies are caused by a combination of physical injury, a temporary or chronic faulty immune system welcoming a bacteria or virus, and an emotional crisis of greater than usual intensity. Over the years I've applied this same philosophy to problems of all kinds and am still surprised at how accurate it is. There are always at least three causes and three remedies for each problem, and often more than three.

This multiplicity of causes and remedies is taken into consideration in this book. It isn't a "one size fits all" book. It helps you find the multiple causes of your compulsion. And it gives you multiple choices for its remedy. It deals with your body and also the three important but invisible factors of your being: your emotional nature, your mental nature and your spiritual self.

As you read, you'll come across moments of logic. However, you'll also notice innumerable ideas that may seem *illogical*. It's my observation that logic doesn't very often get a medal for accomplishment, which isn't to say it will be dispensed with entirely. However, you may already have tried to overcome your compulsion with logic, but without success. Logic is a fluctuating variable from person to person, and from time to time within a person, and from culture to culture or environment to environment. What's logical to me may be on your "worst scenario" list. If you're going to deal successfully with your compulsion, other factors must be called into play. The world is full of people who will tell you these other factors are illogical.

One of the factors is related to judgment. Judgment, more often than not, is a child of your emotional nature and predominating emotional and mental patterns.

Judge not, or be judged, is pretty straightforward advice. Few people realize that on a certain level it also applies to judging yourself. If you begin flogging yourself for the past, as either a reason or an excuse for the present, you're pouring coals on the fire that's already destroying the house. So don't judge yourself by the past.

The future isn't improved by a continuous replay of old hurts and grievances. The future is changed by changing the present. Only by changing the present. And only by changing yourself in the present.

This is not to suggest that you resign as chairman of the board in your life, and simply let come what may. But it is to say that a lot of energy is wasted by playing the same record of regret over and over again. If you're serious about overcoming your compulsion, one of the first steps is to concentrate on today and the opportunities it offers you for regaining the control you once had in your life.

So at this point you may wish to ask yourself a question. "Do I want to stay as I am, or do I really want to be something better than I have been so far?"

Or another question. "Shall I continue to let the past control my future, or shall I control it myself?"

And one more. "Which would I rather be, substandard or exceptional?"

Being something better than you have thus far been is a beginning.

Being exceptional comes later.

And it all begins with taking control of your future by changing the present. And that's a good idea.

What, exactly, is an idea anyway?

If it's good, and energized, it isn't merely a sudden soft breeze that quickly disappears. It's an *energy form* with strength and life. You can literally commune with it, to the extent of sensing its existence, and deciphering the message contained in its vibrational field. It can be absorbed into your own energy field, controlled, loved. You can taste it, inhale it breath after breath. You can plant it in the atmosphere as an energy seed to grow, multiply, and bring forth a harvest after its own kind.

You may wish to consider that the energy idea form to plant at this moment is that others aren't going to re-create you in *their* image! *You are going to re-create yourself in your own image!*

That image isn't the picture of what you are at this moment. Or at any other time during the term of your compulsion. It's the image of your inner, better self which has been waiting for, hoping for, expression in your life.

Do You Encourage Your Compulsion?

There's a subliminal part of you, hidden from normal sight or normal conscious awareness. If you're quiet enough you might hear its plea, "Please. I'm the better you — the *real* you — let me be the image which you and others can see and appreciate."

If you heed and respond to this message from your real self, it will give you more energy-form ideas. For example, it will speak to you about your inner relation to your outer compulsion. It will speak of ideas similar to this:

"My compulsion cannot grow without my permission. In fact it cannot live without my encouragement."

Now here's what may seem a pretty illogical idea. At your next meal, before eating, focus intently on your plate of food for a moment, then speak to it! Mentally say something like this: "You're giving energy to my body, good energy that strengthens and stimulates every muscle, gland and organ. As you do this, you also help strengthen my emotions and mind, my inner being, as well as my body." Then eat slowly, enjoying every energy-filled morsel.

This idea may seem pretty unorthodox. You may or may not wish to try it, but if you do, keep it to yourself. You needn't tell anyone what you're doing. In fact, it will seem totally illogical to most, and they'll try to discourage you. But they'll wonder why you're looking and feeling better. So, if it works — do it!

I'll ask again, "Do you encourage your compulsion?" Each time you give in, you feed it. Every time you feed it, it grows. In what ways does it grow?

It grows in size and content. In degree and intensity of hunger. It grows in capacity to control you. It grows in its skill as a "life-snatcher," actually stealing your life and forcing you out of it.

So you've already struggled against it without results? Intense struggle means that you concentrate your mind and attention on the object of the battle, you feed it. In the cosmic nature of mind and its relation to matter, the principle is that you reinforce and strengthen the object of your constant thought — whatever it is.

Does that mean that if you forget it, it will disappear? Absolutely not. Total forgetting, short of total amnesia, is hardly possible. Forgetting is no more the answer than struggling.

The only way to get one thought out of your mind, including your subconscious mind where compulsions fester and reproduce, is to replace it with another thought which reproduces itself and ultimately crowds out the unwanted trespasser. The only way to get one thought out of your mind is to replace it with another!

Replacement may be a key word for you. Each time a compulsion thought enters your mind, replace it with a different thought — one that has sufficient attraction of its own to become predominant in your consciousness. Bravo! You denied food to your unwanted compulsion. You strengthened your self. And each time you're able to do this you gain ground. You change the future. You earn the right to some additional self respect!

On another level of your life, what's happening when all this occurs? Change — on both the outer and inner areas of your life. The outer is the obvious world around you, tangible to your physical senses. It looks different to you each time you gain ground over your compulsion. And you look different to it, for both your mental perspective and physical appearance are transformed. The inner world is the mysterious world within you, known only to a completely different set of senses, supraphysical in nature, subconscious or supraconscious.

Another view of this change is somewhat inadequately designated as lower and higher. The lower is the physical plane, wakeful level of your conscious awareness. Its values are oriented to the physical origin of your body. The higher is the intangible, seldom used, supraconscious level of your self. Its values are oriented to the spiritual origin of your consciousness.

Multilevel Living Offers Advantages

There are six significant levels of life expression, each of which selfishly tends to draw attention from the others. Like a family with six children, with each child clamoring for attention and pouting or even becoming surly when it isn't received, each of these life expression levels wishes to be foremost. And, when succeeding, any one of these life expression levels glories in the obsessions it creates, incessant clamorings which have their consequences in compulsions and addictions.

If business is conducted on one level only of a six story building, the other five stories gradually deteriorate and the building falls far short of its potential usefulness. So is it with the multitiered life of every human being. Confining the consciousness to one level, ignoring the others, leads to disaster. Giving each level its due leads to freedom from compulsions and addictions, and to a successful, harmonious life.

Physical level thinking cares for your body's needs as a vehicle for life expression. It deserves your attention in making your body the best possible instrument of your inner self. Overindulging its clamor for more than this is self abuse. Its uncontrolled appetites ultimately lead to obvious varied addictions.

Emotional level thinking gives embodiment to tremendously strong energy. Emotional energy, when bottled up or expressed unhealthily, often overwhelms rational thought and goes its own headstrong way. Against seemingly insurmountable odds, athletic teams often defeat other teams of greater physical ability, due to a surge of emotional level thinking. Their emotional energy level stimulates and enables them to run faster, jump higher, push harder, or whatever is required to win over their normally superior opponents. Of all the thinking levels, the emotional most needs to be expressed in a healthy way in order to provide its extraordinary strength in a vital way. You'll want to make use of this strength to overcome compulsions.

Mental level thinking is the level of rational, common sense, logical thought. It's that level of thinking that should be in command, create strategies for winning whether in games, business, relationships, or any of life's activities, important or not. We're all familiar with it and attempt to use it all the time. However, there's a higher thinking level, which, for our purpose, might be termed ...

Upper level thinking. On this level, thoughts are more abstract than concrete. It's the creative level, the level of spiritual yearning, often unrecognized as such by the thinker. It's also the level through which contact with intuition is brought into the vibrational range (or wavelength) with mind as it functions through the brain.

Intuitional level thinking. This little used but marvelous tool of human expression performs a unique function. It "abstracts" and combines information from a wide variety of sources — from all active levels of consciousness, from past experiences, from levels of stored knowledge that exist only in vibrational energy ranges (sometimes referred to as the *Book of God's Remembrance* or the *Akashic Records*) and, through a specialized form of telepathy, from beings both physical and nonphysical.

Spiritual level thinking. Perhaps this is the most difficult of all thinking levels. Through centuries, it has been cluttered and corrupted by overorganized religion, overzealous fanatics, and more than a few avaricious clergy. You must decide what is truly spiritual as contrasted with the demands of organization, fanaticism, and greed. Then your thoughts and life style should progress toward fulfilling the inner yearning and required inner balance for a fulfilling life.

Octaves of Your Life Energy

Just as there are tonal octaves in music, so there are vibrational octaves of your life and consciousness. In music, the higher the audible tone, the higher the octave and the more rapid the vibrations required to create it. Vibrations can be raised through the still higher spectrums of heat and light, then into and through levels of consciousness itself.

Awareness centered upon your physical muscular system and organs is of one vibrational level. But when your awareness is centered upon activities of the emotional and mental type, a higher vibrational level is activated. And a still higher level when a spiritual activity is involved — for example empathy (the ability to sense or feel in yourself what another person senses or feels within him or herself), intuition, love and a relationship, through your own inner divinity, with life's higher spiritual domain. It is important to note here that each level diminishes, to some degree, the levels above it and attempts to function through those below it.

So the theory presented in this book is that you cope with and overcome bad habits, compulsions and addictions by becoming a whole person, always your own person, immersed by and immersed in the Divine Being's energy level. As octaves of your human consciousness become more and more refined, at a certain vibrational range they begin to merge with the Infinite consciousness — and in that context your human being and the Divine Being become one. This is a modern way of understanding the scriptural statements that "I and the Father are one," meaning vibrationally attuned, not meaning the same person. And "I am in the Father and the Father is in me," meaning that my consciousness and the Superior Consciousness, the highest range we can conceive of ("the Father") are similar in nature and responsive to each other. Low C and high C struck simultaneously on the piano keyboard vibrate together without losing their individual qualities. Similarly, it's possible for any level of your consciousness to "become one" with similar levels in both lower and higher vibrational ranges.

All this becomes possible as you learn to manage your own inner environment, and consciously give direction to, and express healthily and with balance, the modulation of your emotional, mental and spiritual vibrational levels. The levels are interactive. When the physical level is properly managed, the emotional and mental levels are improved. When the emotional level is properly balanced, the physical and mental levels are improved. This same reinforcing pattern is activated by and through all the levels: physical, emotional, mental, upper level, intuitional and spiritual.

Is There a Cost?

One way of looking at life is that it's an elaborate barter system. You cannot gain anything on any level of life without giving something in exchange. Everything has its cost. To be rid of a compulsion or addiction you must be willing to pay, not necessarily in money. Time and energy are two forms of payment usually required for overcoming a compulsion or addiction.

You pay good money to support your compulsion or addiction, not counting the cost of their results for which there can be no financial estimate. Look upon overcoming an addiction as an investment. What are the dividends? The successful financier expects dividends on an investment and you have every right to expect the same. But you must determine what you are willing to pay for overcoming the excesses which are causing loss in your life. Not pay in the form of money but in dedication, time and effort. The dividends of dedication, time and effort offer fiduciary returns as well as growth in the value of your own self-esteem, improved relationships, and worth in the workplace, to mention but three areas where your investment provides outstanding returns.

Ever Try a Tobacco Salad?

Some experts believe that addiction to tobacco is deeper and wields the most unyielding grip of all substances. More difficult to overcome, so it seems, and to keep out of one's life, perhaps, than any other. Some stop smoking "cold turkey." Others try anything and everything without success. Perhaps that's been your experience.

There are times when you may need to design your own program, in your own image — times when a creative approach does the trick. For Jess the personally created method has kept him free of tobacco for fifteen years at this writing. I asked him to write the details of his unique method, and they're printed here with a few of my own comments.

Jess's Story

"When I made my umpteeth decision to quit smoking, I wondered how I might do it differently so I would stand a chance of being successful. It came to me that the only way to do this would be to have a reminder of how rank and nauseating tobacco is when it mixes with my body. Since I am mostly water, I thought the logical way would be to mix tobacco with water, and that is just what I did.

"At first I couldn't find a jar for my plan, but then I remembered that the mayonnaise jar in my refrigerator was practically empty. That would be my jar!"

Tobacco, water and — mayonnaise?

"As I added tap water to the jar, I noticed there was about an inch of mayonnaise left. This would be okay, I thought, because my body is not just water, and that I probably should include some sort of organic material that has fat and protein.

"Once I mixed the water and mayonnaise into a clumpy goo, I took the half pack of cigarettes I had left and crumpled them into the jar. I then put the lid back on, gave the jar a couple of good shakes and put it back in the refrigerator. It did look really bad and I vowed to myself that from now on I would have to take a large drink from this jar *before* I smoked a cigarette."

Jess made a vow to himself, a sacred contract. But wait, the addiction hasn't yet loosed its grip. From now on it's a battle.

"It wasn't long before I was at the refrigerator door. After dinner that night, I stood there for a good ten minutes and must have opened it ten times to look at that jar. Remembering my vow, however, I made it through the night.

"The next day was a different matter. All day long I could just taste a cigarette. I thought about it every ten minutes. By dinner I had convinced myself that I should give up smoking more slowly — and that meant I should smoke at least two cigarettes daily.

"This prompted a dash to the store and the purchase of a pack of cigarettes. I remembered my agreement with myself, however, and decided to take my drink before smoking. I knew it would be ugly, but it would be worth the relief."

Is the self-contract losing ground? Should a lapse in the agreement destroy it all?

"I got as far as unscrewing the lid to that jar of revulsion. As I raised it to my lips it dawned on me just how awful and nauseating tobacco can be when it is mixed with water and fat and protein. The smell and appearance of the globs of mayonnaise and water-soaked tobacco were enough to cause my esophagus to constrict in a pulsating rhythm. It was easy to put the jar back along with the cigarettes!

"This went on for several months and I never was able to take a drink from the mayonnaise jar. In truth I kept it for two years before I could simply no longer stand to keep it in my refrigerator. It ended up in my garage and it finally fell victim to being knocked off a shelf just a few years ago.

"As I cleaned up the mess, I realized it represented a triumph over lots of things, not just tobacco, and I knew that my contract/agreement with myself could really extend to other areas of my life. Yes, it was the worst mess I ever had the pleasure of cleaning up."

Jess's insight that one triumph leads to another is an inspiring one. Overcoming an addiction is a king-sized triumph that can easily lead to other, lesser or greater conquests. From top down is one way. From the bottom up is another. Lesser victories can lead to greater ones. It's a win win situation.

Two

Why Stop?

One characteristic of the human being is the often sincere belief that someone else is to blame for his or her compulsion or addiction.

"That's true for others," most persons will say to themselves, "but it just isn't true in *my* situation." Who's to blame? Here's a short list.

Parents, spouse, children, DNA, astrological sign, friends, co-workers, the boss, abuse as a child.

Caught in a web of bad circumstances, been doing it so long I can't change, no one will help me, no one understands me, the time isn't right, had a bad teacher in school, overworked, too much stress, no one will give me a job, the system is against me.

The list might easily expand by a thousand more items. You could go over all of them — and in every instance the honest answer wouldn't tell you who or what should accept the blame for your situation. The reason is that it's a list of excuses. It's a list of truly difficult and complex life situations that should lead you to therapy or to peer group support, but they should not be used as excuses for compulsion or addiction. Giving in to a compulsion or addiction is always a choice. Continuing it is a choice. Life, day after day, is filled with choice after choice.

There's a scripture about choice which I'll paraphrase. A Big Something inside you is speaking. It says, "Listen carefully, my friend, you have a choice — life or death. Choose to live!"

The words "Choose to live," may be as important as any you'll ever hear. Each time you hear, see, feel, smell or taste, you do so out of choice. Every choice, in its own way, contributes to your living or dying. Every choice. No exceptions.

What are you choosing in life? What are you shopping for? What do you really want to buy from life's abundant supermarket of values? If you could stand at the counter and select from life's "goodies," which ones would you consider worthwhile?

Self-esteem, justifiable pride, acceptance by your peers? Attainment of a goal, respect, a worthwhile life, harmonious relationships? They're all there on the counter. You may have any one or combination of them you choose. But there's a price. Quality merchandise is expensive. The price is: choice. Making it, working toward it and, finally, achieving it.

Here's a brief list of compulsions. Which would you choose? They all lead to death in one or more of its several forms, physical, emotional, mental, spiritual. The list: aggression, violence, fear, excessiveness of <u>any</u> kind, negative thinking. Egotism. Gambling, uncontrolled sex, wrong food or drink, theft, lying, abusiveness (of yourself and/or others), trying to please others at all costs, spending, control and manipulation.

Stan's Story

"Stan," I asked a friend, "what made you decide to quit?" (Alcohol) There was a long pause. I could almost see his inner struggle to overcome the reluctance of revealing an intensely personal inner emotion.

He finally answered, "Fear."

I wanted to know what he was afraid of, but fears are truly tender areas of anyone's psyche so I didn't ask. To do something in spite of being afraid may be the most courageous act of all. My hesitation must have given Stan time to summon some determination from a deeply subliminal reservoir.

He explained that he was afraid of what continued abuse might lead to — loss of his job, going into a life of theft, begging, feeding and clothing himself from the inside of half-filled dumpsters, a lingering death from starvation and disease.

"Then," he said, "there was a second step to my decision to quit."

"And that was — ?"

"Pride. What would others think of me — my family, my friends?

"And this," he said, "was followed by a third step, an unusual experience. It was a very special, out of this world moment during which time and timelessness coexisted. For the first time in years I was in a state of true willingness to do *anything* necessary to quit."

Stan's three step decision to stop abusing himself with "outside devices" led to another three step pattern for quitting.

First, he changed the focus of his fear to the gentler but equally persuasive fear that "slipping" would begin the degenerative and destructive process again, into a deeper pit than previously.

Personally, I really think that what Stan thought of as fear (in both his decision to quit and in staying quit) was something else entirely. I believe it was the upward pressure of an *inner area of values*, rising to the surface of his conscious awareness. There's a core of such values deeply embedded in most persons' psyche. Its occasional surfacing may be considered a spiritual experience, for the values aren't necessarily learned qualities; they are inherent to the center of the self, the spiritual nucleus of every life.

In fact, Stan's experience validates this explanation, for the second, almost unworldly step of his quitting, is his connecting with a "higher power." He doesn't name this power, or denominationalize it to make it fit into any man-made mold of an infinite being. It is simply something greater than himself, and more important to him than most anything else. He maintains his connection with it through an inner meditative attitude, inspirational books, group sessions and one on one conversations.

The third step meaningful to Stan is sharing his experiences and feelings "whenever and wherever possible" — without attempt to persuade, simply to share viewpoints which were of help to him.

Sharing experiences and feelings means that you are showing possibilities to others. You are opening doors, and when another person wishes to "walk through," he or she may do so. The idea of opening a door is a mystical inner energizer for the person who does so, Stan in the above illustration, because it touches his own inner resolve. It continues building upon that resolve, reinforcing it as the experience is relived on an inner and higher level connected with Stan's higher self.

It is also a mystical inner energizer for the person who is stirred by the experience and who then "feels" the uplifting power of "passing" (as in an initiation) into a union with supporting energies greater than his own.

In the mystical law that "like attracts like," (stated in the popular idiom, "birds of a feather flock together") Stan has attracted one user at a time to a better expression of his or her own potentials. And each user has contributed to a continuation of Stan's resolve. For this mystical process to work, neither party should make a forceful overt attempt to be a salesperson of his or her own point of view to the other. The spiritual law works better when not interfered with by the exertion of egocentric and aggressive influence.

Quit! When?

There are those who say, "I'll quit on my birthday. On Thanksgiving, or Yom Kippur, tomorrow, or when I get a good job." No date in the future works. There's only one day on which to quit.

Today!

Today is not merely the best day to quit, it's the only day. Put it off once and you tend to put it off again, and again, and again. Today is the day. Do it today.

Quit!

Earlier in this book I stated that if you're caught in the clutch of an addiction you have but one redeeming quality left — your inner potentials. But there is a supporting factor for those qualities in this inner drama of your life. It's the factor that leads directly to your advantageous use of those potentials. Quit because you *can* quit. You possess the potentials. And quit because when you do so a huge and glowing realization of meaningfulness shines in your life.

Compulsions and addictions are behavioral replacements for empty places in the fabric of your life — places where, for one reason or another, huge blocks of meaning have been cut away, leaving an emptiness which no habitual compulsion or addiction can replace.

If you're serious about your compulsive problem, you must do a reweaving job, replacing the rents and cut-away parts of your very soul. But how? The great and glowing opportunity is ever before you.

One of the most inspiring uses of the inner freedom to choose occurred in the life of famed psychiatrist Dr. Victor Frankl. He was a prisoner in a Nazi death camp when a startling revelation burst in upon his consciousness. His wife, parents and brother had died in the ovens. He lived a tormented life with hundreds of others, smothering in a sea of hopelessness. Yet, as this current of hopelessness swirled over them day after day, there were some who were not overcome by it. Dr. Frankl wondered why and was finally rewarded with the revelation that, no matter the *outer* circumstances, *inwardly* there always exists the opportunity to choose the nature of our response. We can continue to give in to the pressure of outside circumstances. Or we can maintain an inner base of self-esteem, a sense of worth as a human being. Those who shared that "worthfulness" with Dr. Frankl enhanced their own self esteem and their connection with the Divine Being in a way which was surely of annoyance to their captors and in a way in which helped the prisoners survive a horrendous situation. They tormented their captors more than their captors tormented them.

You have the opportunity to choose the nature of your response. Are the outer circumstances going to continue to be your captors? Are you going to maintain your sense of self worth as a human being? And become the winner over your tormentors?

Create this picture for yourself. Your compulsion or addiction is your captor, denying you human decencies as well as the countless pleasures of life, particularly your sense of self worth. Free yourself from your captor by quitting. Quit because you *can* quit. Quit because quitting sets *you* free.

Three

What's Real?

Your compulsion is real. Your addiction is real.

"It's all in your mind," say a lot of people. It's more than that, much more. It's in your body, every cell, through the mystical consciousness that resides in those cells. It's in your emotions, through the mystical connection between emotions and mind, influencing all or part of every behavioral act. It's in your mind, tinting every thought with its own muddy color. It's in your spirit, destroying your sense of worthwhileness, excavating a chasm between you and your spiritual self.

You cannot simply run from it by denying its existence. It's not like an army in battle that can "retreat to fight another day." There is no retreat. There's no running away. You win or lose. That's the reality.

Your family and your friends win or lose right along with you. That's also the reality. Family and friends are an organic part of your life, and you are part of theirs. Whatever affects one affects all, in the same way that whatever affects one organ of your body affects others too. At times there may be a chasm between you and your family, friends, business associates and others. It is often true that the chasm can be bridged, relationships repaired, as you progress toward the realization of your goal: deliverance from the grip of your addiction.

At one point in his career, Mickey Mantle was a worldwide baseball hero. But fame is a trickster. She entices you to excess as an aftermath of success. She continually argues that winning her smile is all you need, and that your life will be worthwhile without family, friends, or anything else that matters — except her. She's lying. That's a reality.

Merlyn Mantle, Mickey's wife, and the rest of the family joined him in his compulsive excesses. Without thought of what he was doing, he pulled them in with him. And they chose to go along. Their story has been wonderfully told in Merlyn's book, *A Hero All His Life*. He finally won the biggest game of his life, overcoming his addictions and compulsions, but it wasn't until there were two outs in the last half of the ninth. He died a year and a half later.

"You get to the point where nothing matters," he said on a TV program as he asked the fans who idolized him not to make the same choices he did. "Don't drink and don't do drugs," is the legacy he left for his family and for all the rest of us too.

It's true that you learn by experience. But wisdom says, "How wise it is to learn by *others'* experience!" That's a reality that escapes too many.

At "the point where nothing else matters," reality is invisible. You cannot see it. The truth is that you choose not to see it. At that point only a realization of life's purpose brings reality into focus and makes it visible once again.

The feeding and nurturing of compulsions and addictions is not the purpose of life. They are ways of avoiding purposefulness.

"Why was I born?" is a useful question to ask yourself. Not just because your parents put some chemicals together. That process merely created a body through which you could express your purpose as an individual and unique human being. There are three "higher" reasons for your arrival on earth and incorporating your real self into the temporary vehicle you now embody.

One of the reasons is to express and reinforce the talents that have become part of your being through the ages and through many lifetimes.

A second reason is to acquire and develop new talents to take with you and use in the future.

And the third reason is to pay any debts you owe others whose lives have mingled with your life in both past and present reincarnations. You cannot grow as long as you owe.

Growth of your self, and Self, is the purpose of life.

Becoming more than you have been is the purposeful motivation that fired your entry into physical form.

Becoming more than you are is the purposeful urge that calls upon you to exceed yourself as the years of your incarnation unfold.

Increase Your Worth

Growth of your self is the purpose of life. Not uncontrolled excesses. Not escape. Not denial. Not the avoidance of reality. Growth! Growth of your worth as a human being. And of the merging of your individual values with the eternal values that have always existed, hidden in all cultures, deeply buried and camouflaged in all creeds. That's a reality.

But growth involves risk. To be a worthwhile person, you must be adventurous, willing to take risks. Doing nothing is standing still. Standing still is dying, a few cells at a time.

The first risk is taking control of your life, of being responsible for your behavior. No one's behavior but yours. There's a surprising similarity between taking control of a life plagued with one or more compulsions and taking control of a corporation plagued with losses. The corporation acquires a new chief executive officer (CEO) to turn its fate around and lead it back to the path of success. The compulsive or addictive individual is a failing business and needs the leadership of a new CEO. In the individual, that CEO is the highest element of consciousness he or she can summon to take command. It may be the normal level of mind. It may be the supraconscious level, known to many as the high self. It may be what's thought of as soul or spirit.

Name it what you will, you are the CEO of a corporation unlike any other, a unique blend of spirit and matter: your self and its departments, managers, rank and file workers, purchasing, sales, assets and liabilities, etc. What the CEO does may result in bankruptcy, through continuing loss of behavioral control, resulting in complete worthlessness. Or it may result in personal success, profits and dividends, through the practice of behavioral control policies which reestablish self-worth.

Every good business person is fully aware of the fact that a CEO who thinks he or she knows everything is on the way to failure. The successful CEO learns something new every day. He or she listens to response from top to bottom of the organization. To apply this strategy to a compulsion or addiction ask, "Have I really spent time in 'conversation' with the organs, glands, muscles, nervous systems and blood stream of my body? My emotional nature? My mental or spiritual nature?" It is possible to contact their particular form of consciousness, through engaging in an inwardly controlled meditation, and to receive valuable information for combatting your compulsion or addiction.

Why not take fifteen minutes right now to make yourself as calm as possible — lying down is better than sitting or standing. After you've attained a completely relaxed state, direct the focus of your attention to drift to any body organ you select. Personify the organ as an intelligent entity. Ask what it suggests *you* do to *help it* become a better (perhaps more productive) member of the complete body organization of which *you* are the CEO. Remain quiet for an answer to come to you in the form of a subtle impression. If no such impulse is forthcoming, try the exercise again another time — first attempts may not be successful.

Remember, in attempting this rather mystical procedure you are, in effect, the CEO conducting an interview with a department head, seeking information helpful to the entire organization. You are thinking of your life as a product — your life, not just your body, your life. Your goal is quality improvement. You may be surprised at how many good ideas you acquire through this "inner" method. You can follow a similar procedure, conducting an interview with your emotional, mental or spiritual natures.

In his book *The Eternally Successful Organization*, Philip B. Crosby tells of corporate giants who were humbled by their insistence on conducting their affairs in the same old pattern (the corporate analogy for the compulsion/addiction syndrome). They finally had to obtain new leaders who could replace the corporate compulsions and addictions with better operating methods.

Crosby points out that the success of an organization often revolves around one person, *an intuitive person*, who (inwardly or intuitively) knows what to do and how to do it. In the context of this book, you are that person. And the preceding paragraphs have been describing one of the ways your higher sensing faculties may help you learn what to do and how to do it. You'll find more ideas in this same vein throughout these pages.

The one person around whom an organization revolves, the intuitive person, is the funnel for receiving positive ideas that in turn spread throughout the entire system. In a sense, that person controls the direction taken by the system. Here, we're talking about your life system. Your intuitive nature senses the course that will direct your life to the greatest possible success, beyond the self-serving elements of mind and body.

Paula's Story

Paula smoked three packs of cigarettes daily for twenty-two years before she finally decided to quit. This is the way she did it.

"I allowed stale cigarette butts to remain in the ashtray. When the craving

> was intense, I would lean over the ashtray and inhale deeply. I also went through the motions of smoking a cigarette. I would bring my fingers to my lips, then exhale, and move my hand to the ashtray as if I was placing a cigarette there." The overwhelming stench of an ashtray full of stale cigarette butts, and the realization that *she* must smell that same way to her friends and family, was of sufficient support to her determination to quit. Paula has now been free of her addiction for sixteen years.

You, the real you, the inner you, "flows" through the intuitive funnel of your being into your entire life system. Beyond reason, beyond logic, you possess a psychic intuitive faculty that, properly used, enables *you* to become the central and controlling factor in your body/mind/spirit organization.

In the life-mechanism which you are fine tuning to be addiction-free, there are five important factors under your management (or five departments, to use the CEO analogy). Each of them is important to the whole, just as each body organ contributes to the well-being of the entire body. Improvements, by way of changes, to any one of these five factors, create beneficial effects in the other four.

The mystical human ecosystem rephrases the ancient metaphysical principle and states that life energies attract and influence similar life energies. Actually it's the process of induction. Change the composition of one of the five factors and it stimulates a similar change in the others, just as an electrical current in one wire induces an electrical current in an adjoining parallel wire. Or one magnetized metal induces similar magnetic qualities in another metal. Once the "quitting process" is begun in one factor, it gathers power along with one or more of the others. There is interactive communication and influence between all five of the factors.

The five internal factors of your personal ecosystem are:

Raw Materials — what you eat and drink, what you think, what philosophies you mentally ingest as guidelines, what thoughts and emotions you accept as helpful.

Manufacturing — keeping the equipment in good condition; "the equipment" being your body, mind and spirit.

Distribution — outer points of focus where your energies are spent; home and family, exercise, work, hobbies, volunteerism, etc.

Quality Control — how your energies are used; destruction of self, of ideals and goals, of possessions, of others, or healing and enrichment of these same subdivisions.

Research and Development — the discovery of, or creation of, new "products"; creativity and ingenuity in developing strategies and activities which replace compulsions and addictions.

If you will spend just a few moments with each of the above factors, you will probably arrive at some startling conclusions. First, you *can* make a change for the better in one or all of them. Second, every change, large or small, changes the present and thus also changes the future. Third, every change changes your life. And finally, *you* have control. You're the CEO, whether you like it or not.

As the CEO, conduct an inner "seminar" for your "project managers," the five aspects of your being which relate to the above five factors of your personal ecosystem. Examine each factor for an hour. Think about it, study it, internally resonate with it. Absorb it into every part of your entire being. Decide what steps you want made and take your first steps toward making them. Make a written check list of what is to be done in each department. Check on progress weekly. The good CEO does this — and demands action.

That's real!

Your second most important talent for this job is your use of an inner sense of judgment. Call it intuition if you wish. It should help you decide how to fill in details of the five ecosystem factors. Its decision making is grounded in that puzzling inner self which normally lies dormant, but is often brilliant when called upon.

Your most important talent for the job is control and healthy expression — of your body, emotions, mind — of your total being and environment. Not control of others, but full control and healthy expression of yourself.

That's real!

Four

The Spiritual Way to Deal With Material Problems

There is considerable difference between interest in an activity, or behavior pattern, and a compulsion or addiction to that activity or behavior.

Interest is a mind mode in which you maintain control over your thoughts and actions. This mind mode sends its electromagnetic messages to your brain. Your brain, in turn, allocates them, according to the messages contained in their vibrational nature, to various parts of your body system. The switching system of your telephone company, sorting out the number you want from the millions of numbers around the world, is an analogy for this process.

As long as the communication flow is from your spiritual self through your mind and emotional levels to your body, no compulsions or addictions are possible. When the flow is reversed, body and emotions control mind and spirit, which they dearly love to do, and negative behavior abounds.

So, forget your problem!

Pretty strange advice, isn't it?

Forgetting isn't the *process* of overcoming; it's the goal. Forgetting doesn't take the problem away. But when the problem goes, forgetting helps keep it away.

Indulgence in any kind of compulsion or addiction leads to a kind of life imprisonment. The fullness of your life is taken from your control and given to the problem. The problem is as cold, relentless and restricting as prison bars and walls. You may find yourself confined in this self-imposed prison a few minutes daily, or permanently for the rest of your life. Or you may be free. It's your choice. Depending on your choice, you virtually become your own jailer, ultimately enforcing restraints upon yourself, or your own liberator, opening wide to the fresh, clean abundant air breathed by those who have set themselves free.

You cannot change the past but you *can* change the present and future. This isn't a book about blame, or how terrible a crime it is to have accepted and nurtured a compulsion or addiction in your life. It's about optimism for the future and the better life that results from optimistic and responsible living.

The past need not dominate either the present or the future. It will not do so unless you allow it. And one of the ways to erase the past and its effects on your life is to create an objective. Selecting an objective is an important move toward incorporating your spiritual self in your program to overcome your compulsions or addictions.

Dr. Myron Allen, in his book, *Psycho-Dynamic Synthesis*, says, "The rule of action is to *transmute* your mistakes, not resurrect them."

You cannot change past mistakes, and each time you resurrect them you give them a new inflow of life. When Dr. Allen writes of transmuting mistakes he means to give new direction to the same life energy you've put into the errors. It's done by redirecting the same amount of energy, or more, from compulsions and addictions to the new objective or objectives you select. The moment you take your first step toward a positive objective, you've also taken a step toward freedom from compulsion and addiction.

Selecting and working toward an objective will take your time and energy. It must be worthwhile to yourself and others. Even if you must temporarily allocate resources (mostly time and energy), your expenditure will be a small percent of the amount you're now spending on your negative behavior.

What new objective, or objectives should you select?

An objective should consist of two parts: **WHAT** and **WHY**. The "What" is usually a simple statement such as: "Quit smoking."

The "why" may include several reasons such as "... in order to save my liver, improve relationships with my spouse or partner, and regain my self-esteem," to name but three of hundreds of possibilities.

So create a statement of purpose, set an objective, and you've set in motion some of the most powerful forces, both outer and inner, known to humankind.

What you've done, by choosing the "what" and "why" on your search for freedom from compulsions and addictions, is to create a conscious alignment of your own interior, subliminal forces, or inner energies, with the powerful energy forces of your spiritual self.

The "whys" should be of your own selection and combination. No one can, or should, make selections or combinations for you. The energies involved, should be unique to your own circumstances, needs and aspirations. Your own choices are the only ones that will work well for you. Selecting your personal "what" and the accompanying "whys" supplies the first infusion of spiritual energy on your journey toward freedom from a compulsion or addiction.

To make certain you've made truly helpful selections of your "what" and "whys," apply the following test questions to every statement:

1. Is it simple (so I can easily remember it)?

2. Is it clear (so I can easily understand it)?

3. Is it sincere (reflecting my own true desires and motives)?

4. Does it reflect my spiritual nature (compatible with my belief system regarding spirituality)?

Many think of meditation as vague, useless wishful thinking with religious overtones. In fact, rapidly mounting scientific evidence tells us that the restless mind, unhealthy emotional nature, and the attention grabbing body, are brought under healthy balance through the meditative process. It may, or may not be thought of as "spiritual" by the meditator. But it should be. Meditation is a spiritual device for receiving ideas. To stimulate physical strength on all levels. To motivate the power of will and determination. To organize and coordinate personal activities.

In the context of your objective (what) and its related reasons (whys), there's a special form of spiritual and psychic meditation that will give you insights to propel you toward its realization. Here are a few suggestions you may find helpful:

1. Select a meditation time in advance at least thirty minutes or more. Make an appointment with yourself. Doing so begins the formation of interior thought patterns and connections with higher levels that will contribute to your successful meditation. Do it aloud for emphasis. "This morning at ten o'clock I'm going to meditate on my objective." Keep your appointment without fail. Don't disappoint yourself as a "no show." The consciousness level of body, mind and spirit are thus coordinated to work harmoniously toward your objective.

2. At the selected time, sit upright in a comfortable chair, not the recliner type. Sitting upright helps keep your body and mind active.

3. Relax and breathe easily for at least one or two minutes, letting your thoughts wander at their will. This gives your body time to relax and become subordinate to mental and spiritual activity. Then take absolute control of your thought processes.

4. Focus your attention upon one thought only — your objective. Repeat it mentally or orally several times. When you

notice your mind has wandered away from your objective statement, bring it back under your control by stating it again.

5. Continue Step 4 until you tire of the process, or must fulfill other commitments, then stop till your next session. Do this twice daily at the same time of day, if possible.

IMPORTANT — Have paper and pen ready at hand *before* you begin the meditative process. Three by five cards are excellent for this purpose and have an added advantage: they can easily be carried in pocket or purse and referred to frequently. During most every meditative period, ideas will occur to you to help you overcome your compulsion or addiction. Some of them will be so important and helpful you'll think it impossible to forget them. These swiftly moving ideas, from higher sources within yourself and possibly from outside yourself, caress your mind but briefly and subtly. They'll escape unless you capture them on paper, and review them. Like valued entries on a computer, they must be saved, or they are lost.

In the beginning of your meditative sessions, as brief a time as three to five minutes is sufficient. It may be a new process to which you are conditioning yourself.

Try adding a minute a day until your session lasts ten to fifteen minutes for best results. For most persons that's a minimum. You may wish to increase the time to as much as half an hour. Beyond that time, most persons lose their attunement to the higher energies. They are simply indulging in a state of mental reverie. There's nothing necessarily wrong with engaging in such a lengthy meditative state. The benefits are unique to each individual, determined by personal experiment. (More about reverie in the next chapter.)

The word *spiritual* appears in the title of this chapter. What does it mean?

First, a disclaimer. At least in the context of this book it has no relation to any specific religion or denomination. Religions and their denominations are not broad enough in their scope to include *spiritual* as the word is intended. Here, *spiritual* is a powerful inner feeling which may be found in every religion, or in no organized religion at all. It doesn't depend for validity upon dogma, creed, or any book of religious scripture. Neither does it condemn them. It does not contradict science, though science has yet to discover the degree of its influence upon presently known and verified "natural" laws.

Spiritual — a tremendously powerful inner feeling of a force that transcends the limitations we humans accept at this point in our evolution. It is greater than we are. Yet, by creating the proper body/mind/

spirit relationship we humans can hear its inner voice — and direct its remarkable power in our lives. How?

Ralph Waldo Emerson answered that question with these words, "Silence is the solvent that dissolves personality, and gives us leave to be great and universal."

By silence he meant moments of quietness during which you become one with something greater than you normally are. And in that state you become part of universal spirituality. You are privileged to draw upon it for the thoughts and energies that will help you overcome your compulsions and addictions.

Both meditation and prayer may, or may not, be spiritual. The difference depends upon your own mental state when using either or both of those two procedures.

Janice's Story

Janice is now retired and lives in France. Through many years of a stressful business occupation she became addicted to a number of antianxiety drugs. She says that she attempted to stop using them but it was a disaster. She had to resume using in order to function in her job.

Finally, she changed doctors and followed his advice and his help in withdrawing gradually. Over a period of years she cut down progressively on various drugs as the doctor "progressively reduced the amounts prescribed."

She says, "When I felt ready for the final phase, I took two weeks of vacation in order to move to zero amounts of drugs. For the strong anxiety medicines, there were approximately two weeks of night long nightmares followed by about two weeks of disagreeable dreams which gradually disappeared. I successfully cut out each drug in turn on the first attempt, although this would never have been possible if I hadn't already gone through several months of gradual reduction each time.

Janice continues, "When the withdrawal symptoms were gone, it was a pleasure to feel more clear headed and alert than I had been before taking the drugs in question. It was gratifying to know I had used my own resources and will power to overcome addictive behavior."

Five

Spiritual Synthesis

In the context of helping you improve your life, aided by some of the ideas in this book, synthesis means to include all the elements of your being in a cooperative venture: accomplishing your objective.

If you are to be a whole person, in control of your behavior, master of your life, the process of synthesis aligns and focuses seemingly separated aspects of your self into the kind of functioning whole it was intended to be. *Analysis* is separating a concept or a thing into fragments for better understanding. *Synthesis* is reassembling the parts to create a better whole. These definitions apply to a person (you, of course) as well as concepts or things.

Successful sports coaches emphasize team effort by individuals. Humankind has too long neglected the fact that there are teams within teams, the composition of your inner and higher self being one of them. There is a spiritual side to your nature that should be a working unit in your life mechanism right now. This has little or nothing to do with whether or not you attend the sabbath service of any particular religion, or accept any particular avatar as your personal savior. It pertains to the spirit which is behind all of them. It relates to a vibrational level of consciousness which is unencumbered with the mundane level of life but is at the same time involved in it. It is *in* the world, and *with* the world, though perhaps not *of* the world.

You are the spirit in the cells of your body, and the electromagnetic field within your emotional and mental natures. The Universal Consciousness is the spirit in your mind and soul. The electromagnetic field through which your consciousness expresses, permeates throughout your entire being on all its levels.

Your physical senses keep your mind informed of the external world. In that outer world, however, there is little to help you contend with your compulsions or addictions. But the level of your consciousness which operates in the invisible world, in the higher vibrational level of cosmic perspectives and spiritual synthesis, may provide you with positive, invaluable assistance.

Twenty percent of an iceberg is visible above water. Eighty percent is invisible. Twenty percent of your entire being is visible on the physical level. Eighty percent is invisible and bears several labels — subconscious, super or supraconscious, high self, soul or spirit consciousness, monad, etc. Whatever the name, it's undetectable by physical senses. One comes to an acceptance of its existence through personal experiences with it. If you've not already had such observations or insights, these pages may provide you with helpful direction.

The reality of a benign invisible is a difficult concept for some. Remember, however, that love, in all its varied expressions, is not an energizer only, it's also an energy itself. And love is a benign invisible. Dr. Pitirim Sorokin, famed sociologist, in his book *The Ways and Power of Love*, describes his laboratory experiments at Harvard University. In his laboratory he experimented with love's electromagnetic energy as it is aroused in an individual, and as it is directed to and received by another individual even at a distance from its human generator.

In my opinion, the electromagnetic energies generated by we human beings are more numerous than we realize, and far more powerful. More experiments similar to Dr. Sorokin's are in order. In the meantime we can safely assume there are innumerable invisible energies which you can put to good use overcoming compulsions and addictions.

Determination is an example. How determined are to you to reach your objective? Will you try for one or two days, or a week, then slip back into the old pattern again? Wouldn't it be helpful if you were able to call upon a supply of determination directed to supporting your power of will? This is precisely what I believe you can do through spiritual synthesis.

Individual intelligence is another invisible energy level. Today it may not be scientifically demonstrable. But tomorrow ... perhaps we'll understand the energy inherent in mental activity — the fire in the mind.

While we receive support from others when we meditate together, an important ingredient in spiritual synthesis, as well as spiritual evolvement, is in "going to the mountain" alone. Avatars who go to the mountain for help with their personal needs don't take along a party of followers.

You can establish a meditation period, requiring only a few moments of time, to cause an inner surge of determination, or a stimulation of your mental nature and its synthesis with "higher" intelligence. Set up the meditation in the same way as previously instructed. "Fast from the world" a few moments by dismissing the clutter swirling in your mind. Then let the *spiritual* level of your consciousness "speak" to your body — use your own words to this effect ...

> "Energy of determination, quicken every cell of my body without exception."

For a few moments after this directive, feel the inflow of a new potency in every portion of your body. Then let the spiritual level of your consciousness speak again ...

> "Energy of determination, give support to my emotional nature. Give it strength and stability."

Then for a few moments feel the invigorating charge as your emotional nature responds to the inflow. And for a third time give the spiritual level of your consciousness the opportunity to speak again ...

> "Energy of determination, strengthen my power of will."

Feel your sense of purposeful resolve taking its shape and place in your normal everyday level of consciousness. Continue your inward centering as it flows into every atom of your entire being.

When you feel it is time to end the session, let the focus of your attention shift from the spiritual level of your consciousness to the everyday level again as you withdraw from the atmosphere of the meditative process. During this exit process, express your appreciation for what has been accomplished on the inner, invisible level of your life. Say it aloud if you feel comfortable doing so — or say it mentally. Say thank you — to your own higher self.

> "Thank you for the energy implanted in the cells of my body.
>
> "Thank you for the support given my emotional nature.
>
> "Thank you for strengthening my power of will.
>
> "Thank you for helping me feel good about attaining my objective."

Thank you, in any language, is a magical phrase. When sincerely expressed, it fulfills at least a portion of the mystical (and scientific) law of compensation. Similar energies are more easily expressed and exchanged with one another. Saying thank you does even more. It strengthens the harmonious relationship between physical, emotional, mental and spiritual levels of your own being. It stimulates what could well be termed an interweaving of the energies and consciousness of these levels. It helps the process of your evolving as a whole person in a meaningful existence.

Then, whenever you're tempted to give in to your compulsion or addiction, even if ever so slightly, return briefly to this same meditative procedure. Recreate for just a moment the same inner atmosphere as you consciously focus on the spiritual level of your self. With a little practice, you can revive the inner energies which make you stronger than the outer temptations. You can do so, quietly and quickly, in any situation: in your home, from kitchen to bedroom; on any aisle in the supermarket; on any dark street, in any back alley, or at any gourmet dinner; alone or at a party; anywhere, any time, under any circumstance.

"Going to the mountain" as a spiritual meditative experience is an ancient tradition practiced in all cultures around the world. Many people do not realize that you can go to the mountain even where there is no mountain — in Kansas, or the middle of the Atlantic, in the shadow of a desert sand dune, or the vastness of outer space. And how is that? Spiritual literature speaks to the masses in literal terms. But to the experienced seeker the language is symbolic. "The mountain" is your own higher self! The mountain is your soul or spirit. The mountain is Cosmic Consciousness, or Divine Consciousness. The mountain is; and it is what your personal spiritual belief system accepts.

If the mountain is your own higher self, then there is considerable sense in the statement that "faith can move mountains." In your being there is a spiritual consciousness and there is an every day consciousness. They are represented symbolically by the two kinds of mountains which sacred writings describe — the holy mountain of the higher consciousness, and the stony mountain of the lower. They represent two different states of consciousness — the elevated state of the superior consciousness and the grosser state of inferior consciousness.

The stony mountain (or obstacle) of your compulsion or addiction is your continued satisfaction with the temporary gratification which they provide, regardless of the complications they cause in your life. That mountain can be "moved" (overcome) by the elevation of your consciousness to the higher or spiritual mountain.

Max's Story

Max says, "I owned a butcher shop for 35 years. I became a glutton for food. But they don't call me Buddha any more. I changed because every time I walked by a mirror, I was ashamed. So, I quit eating meat, cold turkey!

"I bought a juicer and it works overtime, juicing everything from A to Z. I am no longer a glutton, addicted to food. Now I have more energy, feel good all the time, and probably added 15 to 20 years to my life. Eating the right foods helps the body cure itself."

You can go to the spiritual mountain in a variety of ways: meditation sessions, prayers, intuitive flashes, directed dreams. And sometimes spontaneous episodes of unknown sources create circumstances which are highly revelational and inspirational.

Occurrences in the not normally conscious area, subconscious or supraconscious, can never be completely understood. The results of spiritual healing, meditation, or prayer, defy exact and undeviating scientific measurement. The measuring tape tells us how far the champion broad jumper leaped. But it doesn't tell us anything about the energized determination in his heart and mind when he set the record. Sophisticated laboratory equipment depicts the quivering protons and neurons which cause their atomic bodies to fluctuate. But it doesn't tell us to what degree the mind and expectant attitude of the one observing these invisible activities has affected the movement.

It's possible that the invisible, not normally conscious area of your self, is one of the greatest helpers in overcoming compulsions. You can enlist its aid by using the very simple process of inner conversation. Get in touch with the invisible level of your life and consciousness by giving it specific, earnest directions. For example, let's say you're going to dinner with friends. Some of them will smoke or drink and urge you to join them. Before you join the group, spend fifteen seconds inwardly speaking to either your sub or supra consciousness. Give it specific directions something like this ...

> "Before I reach for a cigarette, (or a drink, or a shot or pill) tell me not to do it. Tell me why not to do it. Strengthen my resolve not to do it."

Your readiness to receive the spiritual impulse at this moment of temptation creates an alliance with your higher self, your ever ready helper. It brings the spiritual influences into the material maelstrom. It calms the momentary mundane urge, and strengthens your resistance. How good it is!

Six

What Can I Do Instead?

The process of quitting, quite simple though it may seem, requires nurturing just as does a garden, a business, or even any kind of human relationship. How can you nurture the quitting process?

It's an inside job.

A new way of thinking should be substituted for the old, or present, thought process. Ralph Waldo Emerson said, "The secret of education lies in respecting the pupil." He did not mean to coddle the pupil — or be lenient or make excuses for the pupil. Think of how little respect you have for yourself — your body, mind and spirit — when you give in to compulsion or addiction. In the Foreword to this book I described how I despised myself for my addiction. I learned the benefit of substituting a new thought process.

So one way to help educate your way out of bondage, to nurture and strengthen yourself to the point of self-respect, is to remember and follow this maxim:

The only way
to get one thing out of my mind
is to replace it with something else.

Copy this and put it on your refrigerator. Copy it on a 3 x 5 card and carry it in your wallet or purse next to your money. (Your money is one of several areas where your addiction really hurts.) When a compulsive thought arises in your mind, summon the strength to replace it with a different thought. Do it every time, over and over. Perhaps instantly, or possibly slowly, it will help you change the addictive mental energy pattern now superimposed on your brain with the energy patterns of the new thoughts. In time the new will predominate.

Do you remember occasions when a bit of music kept resonating in your mind, annoying you perhaps for hours? Frequently replacing it by controlling, fixing your mind on your daily affairs, finally expelled it from your mental energy pattern. That is a simple illustration of one method for eliminating a magnetic mental urge toward giving in to an addiction.

Neutralize the Magnetism of Your Addiction

Ask yourself, "What can I do that is better than indulging in my addiction?" What will help me regain my health, improve family relations, improve my finances, my ability at work — and above all, my self-respect?" How you answer these questions will offer you some of the most powerful antidotes you can find. Most of them will contribute to your well-being on more than one level, leading to a stronger body, emotional stability, peace of mind and spirit.

To answer the questions in general, there are literally thousands of "neutralizers." Some are better suited to your individual life than others. But the list of possibilities is practically endless. Here are a few "starters" that may nudge you into making a brief list of your own personal and powerful neutralizers.

Sports (swimming, bicycling, an exercise club, coaching)

Hobbies (cooking, photography, sewing, collecting, music, gardening)

Volunteering (hospital, hospice, school, church, community affairs, Red Cross, politics, mentoring)

There are a hundred thousand ways to negate, neutralize and replace addictive behavior. Perhaps the least often considered of all of them may be best for you.

Probably the greatest and healthiest of all substitutes may surprise you. It seems so simple but do not by any means downplay its value. One of the greatest of all substitutes, perhaps *the* greatest, is a simple drink of water. In place of a cigarette, a drink of alcohol, a drug or any other form of addiction, when the impulse occurs to indulge in it — take a drink of water.

Doing so fills more than one need in your life. First, a drink of water satisfies your body in ways that cannot be evaluated. It gives a sense of fullness and thus a feeling that it is unnecessary to indulge.

A drink of water not only satisfies innumerable body urges for sustenance of one kind or another, good or ill, it also will contribute to your health and to your satisfaction of the urge to indulge in your addiction.

If You're Analytical

If you are an analytical person, one who likes to think problems through very thoroughly and from doing so analyze them and thus discover ways to handle them, there is another way you may wish to consider for approaching any compulsive or addictive problem you may have at the moment.

You may wish to look for origins of your problem and various aspects of your problem and how they influence different areas of your being. You will also want to consider various ways to overcome the problems that exist in your life as you perceive them. Here are a few ideas which you will wish to expand upon as a result of your own thought processes.

Think about the specific part of your self in which your compulsive urges originate. Ask questions then, is it in my physical body? In my emotional nature? In my mental nature? In my spiritual understanding?

Remember that nothing will be learned or achieved by placing blame for your compulsive or addictive behavior upon outer circumstances or upon any other person. There may indeed be circumstances which lead you to choose addiction or compulsion. But remember reasons are important to understand and analyze and get some help with, perhaps from a therapist. But the choice of how to deal with them is always yours. The problem is yours and only you can solve the problem. You may need help in doing so, and that will be discussed a few pages further on.

If you determine that the roots of your problem are in your body in some way, what changes will you make in regard to your body?

You will consider the possibility of exercise being of assistance. Perhaps nutrition, what you eat and drink will come into the scope of your consideration. You may consider turning to fasting as an aid. Or to medication. Consider the possibility of your sleep pattern or conditions such as the nature of the room in which you sleep and the bed in which you sleep. Do they have any effect upon you? Do you have the ability to relax body tensions? Become friendly with your body; converse with it and see whether or not it answers your questions.

Consider also that one of the important factors in physical healing is the way you breathe.

A simple daily breathing exercise that can be used in any circumstance is to exhale thoroughly while contracting your abdominal muscles completely. Then slowly inhale through your nostrils while expanding the abdominal muscles until they are fully expanded and you have the feeling your entire chest is full of air. Do this for three to five breaths at one session; it may be done several times daily. This breathing exercise should be specially helpful to extinguish the smoking habit, but useful also in connection with any addiction. This simple exercise will contribute to your well-being on all levels of your life.

There are hundreds of other sources for breathing exercises, and they're probably all good for you. Find the ones you like most and use them over and over.

Perhaps you will determine that the root of your problem is in your emotional nature. To some extent, all are partly rooted here. Which of the following makes you feel better: placing blame for your problem, or examining the situations of your life which brought you to a place of choosing addiction, examining them for helpful understanding and then overcoming them? The way you feel is an expression of your emotional nature. Although very common, placing blame elsewhere is a product of a fractured or immature emotional nature. Overcoming is the result of a unified body/mind/spirit person.

What changes will you make regarding your emotions? Perhaps you will consider meditation in its various forms. One of them would be simply a few moments of quietness and the exercise of your consciousness to create a state of inner calm. You may prefer other types of meditation. For example, use imagery. Create pictures in your imagination that nevertheless have the power of your thought in them. Use the inner light technique of visualizing a powerful light flooding through your entire being, cleansing you of your problem and replacing it with a more positive attitude. Remember that the only way to get one idea out of your consciousness is to replace it with another.

If your analysis points to the roots of your problem being in your mental nature, what changes will you make regarding your mind? Perhaps you will discover that attitude changes are the most important changes you can make. Can you trust yourself to create a list of changes that you should make? Many of us cannot because we're not really aware of our negative attitudes. However in your analytical mode at this time you may acquire an awareness of the negativity of some of your attitudes. And you'll begin overcoming them.

Perhaps you may wish to get help with this process. Professional help is best. The professionals are really trained to help you analyze yourself and make necessary changes in your thoughts, attitude and behavior — help you overcome your problem.

If you wish to use the list making technique, compose a list of your negative attitudes as you understand them. Then select one negative attitude at a time and change it. To help yourself do this use the 3 x 5 empowerment card technique of putting down the exact opposite of the negative attitude on a 3 x 5 card. Carry it with you, put it on your refrigerator or your bathroom mirror and refer to it frequently. Each time you do so reinforces the process.

Within your spiritual self, are you distinguishing the difference between spirituality and organized religion? There is not necessarily anything improper about organized religion, but in some instances it does tend to become calcified. You will wish to break up that calcification and free yourself from it. You may wish to find your spiritual support in a denomination other than the one you know of now, or even an entirely different religion than the one you know of at this moment. Still another choice could be some of the Native American spiritual practices.

You will note that in each of the instances above the question was asked, "What changes will you make?" If you are going to be the analyst then you will certainly arrive at changes to be made. Perhaps you will make changes in your understanding of the situations in your life. Are you beginning to perceive them in a different light, and if so what is that new perception doing for you? The analyst will consider this and many other ideas. Remember that "The Big No - No" is irresponsible behavior. Responsible behavior is an attitude change and in your analysis you will discover it to be perhaps the most important and influential change you could possibly make.

In reading this book there is one rule you should apply as an analyst, and that is "read a book as you would pick fruit from a tree in an orchard."

If you are picking fruit you pay no attention to the leaves of the tree. You simply pick the fruit. Every book contains some material of no interest. Wherever you find it in this or any other book, skip it. Pick the fruit that is ripe for your personal taste and use. Pick the fruit that helps you analyze what you are doing and create the kind of behavior that enables you to overcome your situation at this moment.

The Way of the Spirit

Self-subjugation to an addiction is a millstone in your life, grinding out the last bit of self-respect. Your spiritual nature is following a special "way" that it has chosen. Yielding to an addiction interferes with the journey. Submitting to that interference means that you waive your rightful control over your life. It marks the furthest distance you can get from the place you want to go. It's now time, in your life path, to go beyond your addiction. Your body and lower emotional nature struggle against that idea. Your primal body energy, your higher emotional nature, and your spiritual nature want you to go beyond and overcome it. You choose with which factor you will join. The higher consciousness factor holds the most promise.

At some point there comes a magic moment when you *know* you've tipped the scale in your favor. It will be a moment you will forever savor for its strength and a golden luminescence in your mind.

It's a moment when you will say to yourself, "This is it!" And there will be no doubt. You'll stick to it because you believe it in your soul, in your mind, and every atom of your body. Your entire being will tingle with its music and glow with its light. That's when you'll know you've won. That's when you'll know you're on the way to conquering your addiction. It no longer rules your life.

To help sustain this magical state, use the principle of harmony. Harmony is usually thought of in connection with music, bringing together a variety of musical tones simultaneously that result in pleasing sounds. For other kinds of harmony the principle is the same: a variety of compatible energies are brought together, coordinated and expressed.

In the process of rebuilding yourself as an addiction-free, in-charge-of-your-life human being, one way is to introduce harmonies into the expression of your life energies. The nature of those harmonies will include life expressions and activities of a wide scope. They will include harmonies of the elements of your own being, physical level harmonies that express the greatest well-being possible in your physical life; emotional level harmonies that are balanced throughout the range of your emotional nature; mental harmonies that help you create and sustain an orderly regimen of your various types of thinking processes; and finally, spiritual level harmonies that have no relationship whatsoever to subscribing to the principles of any one religion or the denominational divisions of any one religion. All these are inner harmonies for which you are the composer, director and arranger.

You are in the position of Arthur Sullivan and Adelaide Procter, composers of a remarkable piece of music titled *The Lost Chord*. That outstanding composition tells the story of a musician seated at a mighty organ, idly improvising chords at random until at one magic moment he played a chord so harmoniously remarkable that he was placed in a transcendental state of consciousness upon hearing it. He experienced its tones resonating throughout his entire being. After a few moments the notes died away and he lost the inner and spiritually emotional feeling that accompanied them. Afterward he was not able to discover the same combination of notes that produced the feeling of such transcendence. To struggle to reproduce that feeling may have been an error. To allow it to return naturally at some time in the future would have been a proper "Buddhistic way" of reacquiring it.

Not only are there *inner* harmonies in your life there are also *outer* harmonies. They include relationship harmonies between you and another person or persons. They also include your responsiveness, or lack of it, to the various elements of life you encounter, such as social, occupational, intimate or otherwise.

These outer harmonies in all probability will appear as the result of the inner harmonies you create. The Hermetic principle is: "as above so below, as below so above." For our use in this book we can translate that as: *as in the inner so is the outer.*

One of the ways of overcoming addictions could include your own process of creating harmonies — inner and outer. In doing so, you come face to face with inharmonious situations of many varieties, from personal illnesses and frustrations to relational and vocational problems to spiritual discontent and disillusion. In other words there is hardly an element of your life, even eating a simple meal, where harmonies should not abound. It is not as staggering an undertaking as you might infer from my description. And no one, not even the great avatars, have ever been perfect in the process. You and I can only resolve to practice it to as great a degree as we find possible.

Rebuilding Yourself

When you rebuild a house you don't simply put on a new exterior. You rebuild the inside first, but even before that, you think and plan and ask yourself questions. Why do I want to rebuild this house? What changes do I need to make? How can I improve upon the way it is now?

Can you see that rebuilding yourself into a person free from previous problems, addictions and compulsions, is similar to rebuilding a house? The only place to begin is inside yourself. When that is accomplished, outer improvement automatically begins at once.

So ask yourself — what will I rebuild? How will I rebuild? Make a list just as a contractor would make a list of the various steps and stages in rebuilding a house. Some items on your list might include a few of the following:

Begin every day with a brief period of appreciation, or a few meditative moments.

Cherish every day.

Love every day.

Look forward to every day.

Relish every day.

Have some fun every day.

Do something worthwhile every day.

Share something every day.

Do something unplanned on the spur of the moment every day.

Talk to a friend every day.

Eat an apple every day.

Do not say "I am going to ...." Just *do* it.

Training Your Will

There's a simple and easy way to train your will. Basically it consists of making one decision, and repeating it each day for seven days. For example, if you are a daily coffee drinker, give it up each day for seven days. If you are a daily reader of the morning paper, give it up each day for seven days. If you feel you must watch the news on television daily, give it up for seven days. Follow this routine for several weeks and you will soon realize that you do have much more willpower than you ever thought.

This discipline is what might be called a "minor" exercise. You may or may not return to whatever you excluded from your daily regimen. The exercise is not for the purpose of accomplishing any huge project or realizing any certain goal. It is purely to *practice exercising your will.* Your power of will is something like a muscle. It is improved with exercise. Training your will with these "minor" exercises is similar to training a muscle. The difference is that it is mental rather than physical.

After a very few weeks of these minor mental exercises you will discover they are indeed useful, that you have literally strengthened your ability to use will power in a very purposeful way. Nothing surpasses will power as a resource for overcoming your addiction.

Do Some Freewheeling

In the context of this book, freewheeling might be compared to what is called brainstorming by the Madison Avenue advertising people. They assemble a group, and individuals of the group then think of all the possible ideas which are then listed and considered. There are some rules to this method and among them should be included that no idea is too outlandish to be considered; no judgement should be passed on any of the ideas until they are reconsidered later, or perhaps experimented with at a later time.

No criticism of any idea is to be offered at the time of the brainstorming session.

In this segment regarding freewheeling I want to impress upon you that you should not rely exclusively on someone else to tell you what to do. You possess an innate creativity and imagination, whether you think you really do so or not. Creativity and imagination are part and parcel of every human individual, though many persons do not use those two facets of mind to any great degree. You can do so however to your very great advantage in overcoming addictions and compulsions. In other words, you can use freewheeling to help you quit.

It is quite well recognized that most everyone possesses a judicial mind aspect and a creative mind aspect. The judicial mind dissects an idea and passes judgement on it, is critical of it and often discards it. The creative mind joyfully accepts any idea and begins to expand and extend it to other ideas so that one thought leads to another and sometimes does so with such rapidity that it is almost impossible to put a stop to it. The creative mind accepts with great delight the wildest possible ideas and uses them as an artist might use them in painting great landscapes.

The basis of idea finding lies in consideration of as many ideas as possible. Make lists of them, make notes about them. Never discard an idea out of hand — in other words, never dismiss an idea because it's out of the ordinary or wild. Live with every one of your ideas and make choices only after a considerable amount of experimentation or the passage of time before judgement is made. But how do you obtain these ideas? You might sit quietly for days on end and never think of a single one. But there are techniques that you can easily use for producing the ideas in the first place.

Talk *aloud* to yourself. As you talk let your mind put words on your tongue without restraint of any kind. Produce as many ideas as possible by this method and consider them later without limitation.

Another method of idea producing is to vision yourself helping someone else kick the habit, whatever it may be. What would you tell them? What would you tell them to do, what would you tell them to become, what changes in their lives would you tell them to make? You can probably apply any or all of these ideas to your own situation.

Another technique is to ask questions of yourself — then answer them. For example ask yourself "What can I do to overcome my habit? When should I do it? What changes should I make in myself? In my emotional nature? In my mind? In my habits? In my selection of friends? In the places that I visit?"

Still another technique is simply to take a walk. Aimlessly. Follow your inclination, wherever it leads you, but avoid places that recall memories of situations that led you to your becoming habituated. Make notes of the ideas that occur to you as you are walking, else they will slip easily from your mind.

With all these ideas it is wise to remember that one session may not provide the help that you need. It may be necessary to repeat some of them, perhaps several times, for you to obtain the full benefit of the help they have for you.

And one more technique of freewheeling that could be very helpful to you is to write the problem in a letter to someone you know and in whom you feel safe and can confide in. It can be a family member or a friend. *But never mail the letter*. Include in it all the ideas you think of that will help you solve your problem. Describe how you are going to do it and when.

Don't rely upon someone else to tell you what to do. Rely upon that part of your consciousness that is totally familiar with your problem and what to do about it. Do some freewheeling and bring the solutions from that other part of your self into your conscious mind and your everyday life.

What words do *to* you — And can do *for* you

You often think in words — but that is merely the beginning of the story. Your body reacts chemically, emotionally and mentally to specific words. Your reaction differs whether the words are verbal or printed, or created by watching television, listening to the radio, or connecting with any other source of those words. You react differently to verbal slurs, for example, than you do to compassionate, inspirational words. This fact presents you with an excellent opportunity to use words as a resource for overcoming your addiction or compulsion.

Your choice of words that are positive in nature, and meaningful to you and you alone, may be of tremendous assistance as a powerful inner resource.

Even words written in notes to yourself, though not heard by any other person, can cause the same positive responses as spoken words. In a series of seminars I've conducted throughout the world for more than 35 years, people have been helped to progress in their vocations, their avocations and in overcoming their addictions to negative attitudes and ways of life, through selecting a single word as an aid to the process.

The way to do this is to select one significant positive word and make it the underlying thought of your life expression for one week. The following week select another word that will also contribute to the positive tenor of your life expression. The word you select should be written or printed in letters as large as possible on a 3 x 5 card. The card then should be taped to your refrigerator, bathroom or bedroom mirror — and another card with the same word carried in your purse or wallet or taped to the dashboard of your car. This embosses it on your sub- or superconscious mind, or both.

Those two higher aspects of your persona will frequently remind you of your goal. And more than that, they will work 24 hours daily to help bring it about. They will attract people and situations into your life that will help you attain whatever goal you have chosen. They will strengthen your own resolve. They will trigger fresh inspiring ideas of your own creation. But you cannot leave it entirely up to those higher, though resourceful, aspects. You need a plan.

What goal do you want to attain? State it in one word if at all possible. The simpler it can be stated the easier to remember it, repeat it, and reinforce it. Thus, easier to attain it.

It will also be helpful if you will answer for yourself this question; "What am I willing to do to attain my goal?" The question is valid for every kind of goal-setting and attaining. The athlete decides upon how much and how strenuous training he or she is willing to engage in to reach the athletic level set as the goal. The chess player determines the amount of time he is willing to devote to study the game. The writer selects how much time to give to practice writing. And it is the same through every human pursuit. The price to pay equals your own dedication.

Do not — I repeat, do not — select a goal that can be attained only if *others* change *their* lives. It is your responsibility. You select the goal. Your higher consciousness helps you attain it.

Writing a lengthy description of your goal can be complicated. It is better to put the goal in one word only. Doing so focuses your inner faculties like the concentrated beam of a laser.

Remember, select one word only and let your mind dwell upon it frequently but briefly for one week. It is not necessary, in fact it may be counterproductive, to be intense about the word. It should be subtly but fully woven into the fabric of your life. It need not, in fact should not, prove dominant over all other thoughts you may have during the week. Realize that body, emotional and mental reactions to a single word powerfully affect every muscle, gland and organ (and possibly even the bones) of your body as well as your general emotional and mental attitude.

Here is a suggested list of words from which you might wish to choose over the time you do the exercise. Remember to put them on 3 x 5 cards, no more than one word each week. With this list and just a very few more you will have enough to last for a year should you really need that amount of time. Remember, use no negative words whatsoever.

Affection

Alertness

Appreciation

Awareness

Balance

Cheerfulness

Cleanliness

Compassion

Concentration

Confidence

Contentment

Cooperation

Courage

Courtesy

Dependability

Determination

Devotion

Diligence

Discernment

Discrimination

Discipline

Energy

Eloquence

Enthusiasm

Faith

Forgiveness

Fortitude

Friendliness

Generosity

Gentleness

Honesty

Humility

Initiative

Integrity

Joy

Love

Patience

Perseverance

Responsibility

Serenity

Sincerity

Steadfastness

Tranquility

Will

Wisdom

Oscar's Story

Oscar wrote: "I had been smoking cigarettes for about eight years and began to consume two packs a day. In those days, long before warnings were published on cigarette packs, we used to jokingly refer to cigarettes as 'cancer sticks' and 'coffin nails.' It didn't require much common sense to know that smoking was injurious to one's health. I frequently thought about giving up the habit.

"One morning, after arising and dressing, I reached for a new pack of cigarettes lying on top of my dresser. Suddenly and unintentionally, at that moment, I decided then and there to give up smoking 'cold turkey'.

"Acting on an impulse, I cut a half-inch strip of white paper and wrote the day, month, and year on it. Next, I taped the dated strip of paper horizontally across the unopened pack of cigarettes and placed the pack in a prominent place on my bookcase shelf where I could easily see it. As I gazed at my handiwork from across the room, I thought '... the cigarette pack looks like a tombstone!' I had symbolically buried my cigarette habit. I remained determined to stop and discovered that the torturous craving for cigarettes lessened within a week but the desire to smoke was still with me. At the same time, I put aside the money that I would have spent on cigarettes and decided to spend it each week on a new record album as a reward for myself. I looked forward to the weekly record purchase and eventually accumulated a very large record collection.

"One day, many months after I had quit the habit, my Dad was out of cigarettes and in desperation to obtain a smoke, he opened the pack on my bookshelf and lit one up. His conscience later bothered him over this act and as a result he also was able to quit smoking cold turkey.

"This all occurred over almost forty years ago and I have never smoked since that memorable morning. I never had any help although I suspect that I received some from the spiritual side of life."

In the mystical language of spiritual scripture of most every religion it is stated that "in the beginning was the Word." It implies that a higher energy becomes involved in bringing order out of chaos. In a very personal and uniquely individual way that is what happens when you create the vibrational essence which accompanies the words you select as meaningful in your life. You are in fact bringing order out of chaos.

If you need additional word selections, a book of synonyms will offer you scores and scores of words that can be used in this same manner. Remember, those I've listed constitute suggestions only. Words do things *to* you on every level of your life, and you can use them to do things *for* yourself to accomplish whatever you wish to do.

Seven

Use Your Subconscious Mind

My friend, Les, told me of the unusual way which he used to promote his quitting smoking. This is what he said:

Les's Story

"I asked myself how much I would pay not to smoke a cigarette. I decided that $100 was the amount.

"Then I told my sister that I would pay $100 if I smoked a cigarette in two days. After that time elapsed I would smoke again. Then I agreed to pay $100 if I smoked during a longer period of time. I never felt that I was withholding anything from myself, and knew I could smoke at any time I chose to do so. In time, it became months, and then, eventually, I didn't feel like smoking anymore.

> "Among the benefits that I derived from stopping were that it also gave me the strength to stop drinking beer and liquor. Stopping also awoke a discipline within me which has served me well ever since."

Many years ago a friend of mine named John Williams, an expert on health issues, wrote a book titled *The Knack of Using Your Subconscious Mind*. Here is a quotation from that book.

"The subconscious mind is an extremely efficient and dependable working partner, capable of solving many of our most baffling problems and of creating bold new ideas for our personal growth and progress."

Your subconscious mind actually is purely a function of your total mind, just as a muscle is a function of your total body. It will atrophy just as does a body muscle if you do not use it.

Your conscious mind makes the decision to quit. Your subconscious helps you do it.

Your conscious and subconscious are *both* functions of your total mind. However the subconscious is rarely recognized or encouraged. So if you will recognize and encourage it, it will serve you almost beyond belief through the rest of your life.

Now something unbelievably simple regarding your subconscious, another brief quotation from John Williams' book: "The first requisite of creative mental life is, therefore, positive thinking. Aspiration molds the mind in a stronger way than does fear or trepidation. Appreciation is more creative than aversion. Confident thoughts are more powerful than questioning doubts. It is by thoughts of high desire and hope — emotions that are courageous and inspiring — that we achieve more abundant and creative living, a more harmonious inner state and a more commanding personality."

Anything that you place in the subconscious, using mental repetition, is enhanced by your belief and persistence. There are many who recommend writing your goals in complete detail. It is simply a personal opinion of mine that lengthy goal writing can be a complicated exercise. However, if that is a preference I find no fault with it. It is also my opinion that writing goals using only one word focuses the subconscious on that goal like a laser concentrates scattered light into a single beam. It is for that reason you were given words in a previous segment, single words only, that can serve as goals for a variety of ways of overcoming addictions/compulsions. Remember, your consciousness chooses the goal, your subconscious helps you attain it.

The Greatest Opportunity You Will Ever Have

Opportunities for success in life arrive with startling frequency when you recognize what they are — and take advantage of them. Of such opportunities perhaps the greatest of all is the realization that you possess the power of choice.

You were born with that power, exercised it from the moment of your first breath, through the years of your adolescence, and it became the measure of your graduation into adulthood. Choice is an opportunity — and a power — in your life at this very moment. Never believe you don't have a choice. Never even think it. You always have a choice.

Furthermore — each choice is a cause and creates an effect. It's an expression of an immutable and universal law. Addictions, from the smallest to the largest, either succumb to the choices you make or grow from them with a ravenous appetite.

Every cell of your body is influenced by your choices. Remember that "energy follows thought" and "the nature of that energy corresponds to the nature of the thought." Every surge of your emotional nature is propelled and powered by your choices. Every expression of your will, or lack of it, is a child of your choices and a parent of your future. Quit!

Choosing to quit is no small matter. It may or may not be easy. Neither is the choice of when to quit. Let's examine these two aspects, enabling you to cease being the slave of an addiction or compulsion.

Quit to reclaim your life and your self. What you are doing is choosing mind and spirit over body, life over death.

You can make this choice you'll be proud of, or the choice you'll regret. Your choice will either make you vulnerable or put you on solid ground. You can choose the easy road to failure or the hard road to success. No one says it will be easy, but — it is *simple.*

Every effect has its cause, or probably combination of causes. In today's world *external* causes abound. Combined with the negative *internal* variety, they proliferate like mosquitos on a stagnant pool. If you choose to remain stagnant, your life, and the lives of others, will be miserable.

But you can change it all if only you will choose to do so.

Make the choice to change your attitude.

Make the choice to change your action.

Make the choice to QUIT.

Then QUIT.

The publisher of this book is a nonprofit organization presenting metaphysical, mystical, philosophical and self-help material. For more information on Astara or additional books by the author, write:

Astara Administration Building
P.O. Box 5003
Upland, CA 91785

E-MAIL: **mail@astara.org**

WEBSITE: **www.astara.org**